THE BUSINESS OF PEOPLE

SAGE was founded in 1965 by Sara Miller McCune to support the dissemination of usable knowledge by publishing innovative and high-quality research and teaching content. Today, we publish more than 750 journals, including those of more than 300 learned societies, more than 800 new books per year, and a growing range of library products including archives, data, case studies, reports, conference highlights, and video. SAGE remains majority-owned by our founder, and after Sara's lifetime will become owned by a charitable trust that secures our continued independence.

Los Angeles | London | Washington DC | New Delhi | Singapore

THE BUSINESS OF PEOPLE

THE SIGNIFICANCE OF SOCIAL SCIENCE OVER THE NEXT DECADE

CAMPAIGN *for* SOCIAL SCIENCE

Los Angeles | London | New Delhi
Singapore | Washington DC

CAMPAIGN for **SOCIAL SCIENCE**

30 Tabernacle Street
London
EC2A 4UE
+44 (0) 20 7330 0897

Los Angeles | London | New Delhi
Singapore | Washington DC

SAGE Publications Ltd
1 Oliver's Yard
55 City Road
London EC1Y 1SP

SAGE Publications Inc.
2455 Teller Road
Thousand Oaks, California 91320

SAGE Publications India Pvt Ltd
B 1/I 1 Mohan Cooperative Industrial Area
Mathura Road
New Delhi 110 044

SAGE Publications Asia-Pacific Pte Ltd
3 Church Street
#10-04 Samsung Hub
Singapore 049483

Typeset by: C&M Digitals (P) Ltd, Chennai, India

© Campaign for Social Science 2015

First published 2015. Published in collaboration between Campaign for Social Science and SAGE

British Library Cataloguing in Publication data

A catalogue record for this book is available from the British Library

ISBN 978-1-4739-1882-5

At SAGE we take sustainability seriously. Most of our products are printed in the UK using FSC papers and boards. When we print overseas we ensure sustainable papers are used as measured by the Egmont grading system. We undertake an annual audit to monitor our sustainability.

Contents

Foreword

The Campaign for Social Science was set up in 2011 to inform public policy, build coalitions and engage in measured advocacy. It sprang from the Academy of Social Sciences, whose thousand Fellows are eminent academics and practitioners in business, government and civil society; 47 learned societies are also members, representing 90,000 social scientists in varied settings. In this report we showcase the economic and social dimensions of UK science today and look forward to tomorrow with recommendations for this and the next government to consider.

At the 2015 Westminster elections and through the spending review that will follow, the Campaign has a robust case to make to the Treasury, ministers, MPs and policymakers. Research, data collection and education and training in social science must be sustained. On them depend innovation, productivity growth, civic resilience and much more. Without adequate investment the UK loses.

This report summarises for a wider public what social scientists are doing in its midst. The business of social science is what people do and how they behave, as citizens, consumers, producers and holders of opinions: it's them we seek to understand, 'nudge' and explain.

Large problems – call them challenges or opportunities – lie ahead. Whatever the election outcome they will go on demanding the skills and imagination of well-trained social scientists. Whether we look abroad to regions of conflict or within the UK to divergent claims on state and nationhood, whether we think about flows of capital and people between nations or new modes of exchanging data over distance: social science brings an accumulated stock of knowledge and characteristic methods of inquiry to understand and deal with our world.

It does so in collaboration. The challenges of the next decade will demand evidence and insight from social scientists working in new ways with colleagues from the natural sciences, engineering, arts and humanities. Much of Sir Mark Walport's first annual report as Government Chief Scientific Adviser (GCSA) reflected studies on risk, uncertainty and enterprise by social scientists. It's with confidence in the necessity of social science that the report stakes its claim on scarce resources.

We would like to thank all those who have devoted time to the project. Particularly the Working Group, who shaped its conclusions. Also the Review Group, chaired by Paul Boyle, who were enlisted to prevent us straying too far from good sense, though they are not responsible for our conclusions. We are very grateful to SAGE for publishing the report;

also to the Joseph Rowntree Foundation, British Sociological Association, Regional Studies Association, British Psychological Society, Nuffield Foundation and Royal Statistical Society for their support.

We are launching *The Business of People* in February 2015, and will use it as the basis of our advocacy on behalf of the social sciences through the general election, spending review and beyond. We also plan to take the report on a roadshow to more than 25 universities. If you would like to join the Campaign to support and strengthen our efforts, please do get in touch.

James Wilsdon
Chair, Campaign for Social Science
policy@acss.org.uk

Working group

James **Wilsdon** (Chair), professor of science and democracy, University of Sussex; **Simon Bastow**, senior research fellow, LSE Public Policy Group; **Claire Callender** FAcSS, professor of higher education policy, Birkbeck and UCL Institute of Education, London; **Diane Coyle**, head, Enlightenment Economics and former Vice-Chair, BBC Trust; **Will Davies**, senior lecturer in politics, Goldsmiths, University of London; **Charlie Edwards**, director of national security and resilience studies, Royal United Services Institute; **Sally Hardy** FAcSS, chief executive, Regional Studies Association; **Michelle Harrison**, chief executive, TNS BMRB; **John Henneberry** FAcSS, professor of property development studies, University of Sheffield; **Heather Laurie**, director, Institute for Social and Economic Research, University of Essex; **Melissa Leach**, director, Institute of Development Studies, University of Sussex; **Ziyad Marar**, global publishing director, SAGE; **Helen Margetts** FAcSS, director, Oxford Internet Institute, University of Oxford; **Daryl O'Connor** FAcSS, professor of psychology, University of Leeds; **Jane Pilcher**, senior lecturer in sociology, University of Leicester; **Michael Reiss** FAcSS, professor of science education, UCL Institute of Education, London; **Andy Ross**, director, High Oak Enterprises and former deputy director, Government Economic Service; **Sue Scott** FAcSS, honorary professor of sociology, Centre for Women's Studies, University of York; **Hetan Shah**, executive director, Royal Statistical Society; **Pat Thane** FBA, research professor in contemporary history, King's College London; **David Walker** FAcSS, head of policy, Academy of Social Sciences; **Neil Ward** FAcSS, pro vice-chancellor, University of East Anglia.

REVIEW PANEL

Paul Boyle FAcSS FBA (Chair), vice-chancellor, University of Leicester and former chief executive, Economic and Social Research Council (ESRC); **Sir Charles Bean**, former deputy governor, Bank of England and professor of economics, London School of Economics; **Colin Crouch** FAcSS FBA, vice-president, British Academy and emeritus professor, Warwick Business School, University of Warwick; **Sir Andrew Dilnot**, warden, Nuffield College, Oxford and Chair, UK Statistics Authority; **Dame Janet Finch** FAcSS, former vice-chancellor, Keele University; **John Goddard** FAcSS, emeritus professor of regional development studies, Newcastle University; **Dame Jil Matheson** FAcSS, former National Statistician; **Sir Peter Scott** FAcSS, professor of higher education studies, UCL Institute of Education, London; **John Urry** FAcSS, distinguished professor of sociology, Lancaster University.

Executive summary

The challenges facing the UK – its prosperity and functioning as a place for trade, creativity, exchange, equity, and opportunity – will be met only if we deploy social science knowledge, skills and methods of inquiry ever more intensively. To thrive we must innovate. In innovation, we must marry progress in technology and the physical and life sciences with insights from studying behaviour, place, economy and society. To exploit the vastness of Big Data emerging from social media, the biosphere, health and public administration we need collaboration across the disciplines.

Advancing and applying science depends on profits, policies, markets, organisations and attitudes. These are social science themes. In *Our plan for growth* (the science and innovation strategy published in December 2014), the government underlined the necessity of deploying 'all the sciences'. Within this mix, social science supplies tools, concepts and models to help us think about and run the state and markets.

We join with colleagues from other disciplines in calling for more public investment in research. The advance of knowledge is a precondition for prosperity (and the tax revenues it supplies).

UK research enjoys high international standing, to which social science makes an impressive contribution. UK-based social scientists deliver disproportionately to their numbers and funding, as attested by global citation indices and benchmarking reviews. The results of the 2014 Research Excellence Framework (REF) show the enduring quality of the UK's world-leading individuals and departments in the social sciences and such top-ranking institutions as the LSE.

As in 2015 it celebrates its 50th anniversary, the ESRC must be financially equipped to contribute to cross-disciplinary programmes while supporting training and at least maintaining – if not improving – the proportion of alpha-rated research proposals it can fund. Social science capital investment projects (for example longitudinal and consumer data) deserve greater prominence in the government's 'roadmap' for future investment and must be sustained.

RECOMMENDATIONS

1. Investment

1.1 The 2015 spending review should ring-fence the budget for science and innovation and pledge real terms growth of at least 10 per cent over the lifetime of the next parliament.

1.2 This additional funding should be dedicated to interdisciplinary research and cross-council programmes.

1.3 Further iterations of the government's strategy for science and innovation must recognise the contribution of social science more explicitly, particularly innovations in organisational processes and productivity derived from social science and its role in understanding the nature of innovation itself.

1.4 We urge the Treasury and HM Revenue and Customs (HMRC) to examine how the Research and Development (R&D) tax regime might better recognise and support social-science-derived innovations in organisational process.

1.5 We welcome the recognition of social science in the capital investment roadmap and urge the next government to continue support, both revenue and capital, for the internationally acclaimed birth cohort and longitudinal studies.

2. Research priorities

2.1 We urge the Nurse Review of the research councils to recognise the indispensable contribution of social science to cross-disciplinary, problem-focussed research, to push further strategic coordination between the research councils, and to build on the 2014 Triennial Review's endorsement of the ESRC's leadership in and support for collaborative work.

2.2 The ESRC share of the research council budget must better reflect its value for money, support for excellence and promotion of impact, as attested by the 2014 REF results.

2.3 The ESRC must be equipped to support work on the challenges up to 2020 described in this report, including innovation in collecting and analysing Big Data and new forms of data.

2.4 The UK's capacity for interdisciplinary research is a great asset in international collaboration and the new £375 million Newton Fund should give priority to projects that bring together natural and social scientists and engineers to work with counterparts in the emerging economies on shared social and environmental challenges.

3. Other funding points

3.1. The dual support system for scientific research and scholarship should be maintained, recognising the critical role of Quality-Related (QR) funds in maintaining excellence and diversity in social science.

3.2. University leaders and social scientists must ensure, within individual universities, that QR funds intended to support social science reach their target.

3.3 We recommend that in preparation for the next research excellence exercise, the funding councils allow researchers to submit outputs to more than one assessment panel, in order to support interdisciplinary ways of working.

3.4 Beyond the ringfenced science budget, Whitehall departments and the devolved administrations should sustain investment in social science research and data. Resources available to the Office for National Statistics (ONS) and the devolved statistical agencies should reflect their prime importance in providing quality-assured socio-economic data and analysis.

4. Students

4.1 Loans for taught master's degrees must ensure fair access across the social sciences, and social science expertise should be applied in evaluating their effects on social mobility, labour markets and meeting strategic needs.

4.2 The next government should keep international students out of any targets to reduce net migration and reintroduce an option for non-EU graduates to stay in the UK to work for up to two years.

4.3 Building on such initiatives as the Q-Step Centres, social science education must increasingly equip the next generation of researchers with quantitative techniques, the capacity to acquire and analyse new forms of data and the disposition to collaborate with other scientists.

5. Strategy

5.1 The Government Chief Scientific Adviser (GCSA) should produce a new strategic framework for the social sciences, encompassing research, data and the supply of trained people to meet the needs of individual disciplines, business and government.

5.2 The UK Strategic Forum for the Social Sciences should be reconstituted to support the GCSA in preparing this framework, by gathering evidence and monitoring the pipeline of social scientists moving into business, government, the universities and research.

5.3 Areas of strategic priority for the next five years include data skills, macroeconomics and equipping more social scientists for collaborative working across the disciplines.

6. Data

6.1 Strategy must embrace collection and analysis of data by the ONS and the devolved statistical agencies, the decennial census, the UK Data Service and other ESRC resources, and the commissioning of surveys by Whitehall departments and the devolved administrations in the context of policies on open and shared data.

6.2 We urge the next UK government to carry forward the Cabinet Office's work on creating a statutory presumption in favour of sharing de-identified public (administrative) data for research purposes.

7. Government and social science

7.1 At Westminster, the Prime Minister, Cabinet Secretary and GCSA need a 'chief social scientist' to supply wide social science perspectives on institutions, behaviour and data.

7.2 We urge more Whitehall departments to appoint candidates from social science backgrounds as their chief scientific advisers and correspondingly encourage more social science researchers and practitioners to put themselves forward for appointment.

7.3 Departmental science advisory committees should be enriched by the appointment of more social scientists.

7.4 Arm's-length bodies and local authorities, especially in big cities, should review their use and commissioning of social science knowledge and evidence.

7.5 Social scientific advice to the Westminster parliament and the legislative bodies in the devolved administrations should be strengthened, as part of broader modernisation of scrutiny and the supply of evidence.

PART I
SOCIAL SCIENCE NOW

INTRODUCTION

UK parliamentary elections this year and the spending review to follow pose tough questions, at home and abroad. Debates about how to manage public finance, reshape taxation and spending and boost productivity, training and returns to skills all sit under the overarching question of how to organise the state and markets to realise the maximum potential of individuals and communities. How diminished would public and policy debate be without the Institute for Fiscal Studies (IFS), a leading example of applied social science?

After the referendum in Scotland the distribution of power between centre and locality is fluid. Questions about the constitution intersect with UK membership of the European Union, which, for many, pivots on migration and the pace of economic and social change, both at home and globally. Add intergenerational justice and the relative claims of young and old, gender and sexuality, regional instability, terrorism, online data and, last in this sequence but evidently not least, climate change – where understanding attitudes and behaviour is as challenging as the physics. All the above are first-order questions for social science researchers and practitioners.

The research councils call for 'novel, multidisciplinary approaches to solve big research challenges' such as the digital economy, energy, food security and lifelong health and wellbeing. Whether compiled by government horizon scanners, corporate strategists or consultancies scoping sales and investment, such lists have one thing in common. No theme can be addressed through a single body of knowledge or discipline, certainly not just by 'science' as it used, narrowly, to be defined. The goal has to be *diversity of knowledge* in which understanding markets, behaviour and attitudes (towards new products and processes) matches technological and research breakthroughs.[1] As Sir Mark Walport, the GCSA, puts it in his annual report for 2014: as we learn how to modify our physical environment we build social and economic structures, and we must invest in understanding their sustainability.[2]

SOCIAL SCIENCE IS CENTRAL TO 'SCIENCE'

The UK is predominantly a service economy in which comparative advantage is held by insurance, finance, communications and business services, as much as pharmaceuticals or aerospace. Growth depends on these sectors innovating and improving productivity. Yet if 79 per cent of gross value added comes from the service sector, only 8 per cent of business services firms have cooperative agreements with potential suppliers of insight into organisational performance, indicating the scope for productivity enhancement.[3]

Social science has to be recognised as central in combating infectious disease. For the World Health Organization and donors, the Ebola crisis in West Africa demands clinical expertise, better understanding of pathogens and investment in drugs. But defeating disease also hinges on better understanding people – those highly complex animals – and their communities. As well as doctors and nurses the campaign needs experts in how attitudes (towards hand washing, say) are shaped, along with specialists in administration, in markets and drug pricing, in why states fail and how they might be rebuilt and, delicate but profound, how leadership and funding structures can create and sustain the dedication of doctors and the courage of nurses.

This is why the Ministry of Defence (MoD) (to take another example) looks to BAE Systems plc and other suppliers for military hardware, but also to social scientists in thinktanks and universities. In the words of Rear Admiral John Kingwell, head of the MoD's Development, Concepts and Doctrine Centre, no security and defence challenge will be addressed simply by armed force: 'we really need to invest in understanding the world'.[4]

TOWARDS A STRATEGY FOR SOCIAL SCIENCE

Such knowledge is nurtured in a rich ecosystem of teachers, trainers, disseminators, researchers and practitioners, communicating through learned societies and journals, reflected in Figure 1.

As well as continuing investment, the UK would benefit from more *strategic thinking* about the contribution of the social sciences. The GCSA should produce a strategic framework for the social sciences, encompassing research, data and the supply of trained people. Areas of strategic priority for the next five years include data skills, macroeconomics and equipping more social scientists to collaborate across the disciplines.

Figure 1   The size of the research community in social science

In 2010–11	000s
Academic and research staff in social science departments, engaged in research	30.5
Estimated number of professional staff with social science qualifications working on translating or mediating social science research	
Government and public services	177
Finance institutions and banking sectors	169
Consultancy	38
Total estimated staff in translation/mediation work	384
Total population of social science 'research community'	*410*

Source: Bastow et al., *The Impact of the Social Sciences*, SAGE, 2014, p. 274

Some years ago Sir Alan Wilson recommended broadening the scope of the Strategic Forum for the Social Sciences.[5] This should be reconstituted to support the GCSA in preparing the new strategic framework, by gathering evidence and monitoring the pipeline of social scientists moving into business, government, universities and research. The Strategic Forum should bring together government, including the devolved administrations and arm's length agencies, the big charities, the ESRC, the ONS, the Academy of Social Sciences and the British Academy, with lines to the devolved administrations. Strategic thinking is particularly required around data, joining collection and archiving with improved quantitative skills and opportunities for innovation and cost effective public service delivery (through the exploitation of administrative data).

Within Whitehall, cross-government thinking about demands for evidence and analysis should extend to training, data and international research collaboration. Supply is a pressing theme. Social science students extend the talent pool for data analysis and interpretation. Improving their quantitative and analytic skills is a task for the universities, learned societies, national academies, the Department for Education (DfE), the Department for Business, Innovation and Skills (BIS), the devolved administrations and the Nuffield Foundation (which has instigated the Q-Step programme, supported by the ESRC and the higher education funding councils). Loans for taught master's degrees, agreed by the coalition government, must ensure fair access across the social sciences. Social science expertise is needed to evaluate costs and the effects of the policy on, for example, social mobility and earnings and in meeting strategic needs.

THE FUTURE IS CROSS-DISCIPLINARY

Social science is collaborating ever more closely with computing, mathematics, the life and physical sciences and engineering; cross-disciplinary work is becoming the normal way of understanding the world. Comprehending markets, customers, products, competitors and employees is a precondition of commercial success, says Anand Anandalingam of Imperial College Business School, welcoming KPMG UK's £20 million investment in a centre of advanced analytics, drawing on engineers, computer scientists and specialists in 'social arrangements', inside and outside business firms.[6] Social scientists cooperate with clinicians in health, and with geologists, biologists and operational research specialists. An instance is the Wellcome Trust award to Sarah Cunningham-Burley and Anne Kerr to examine how cancer patients and their carers and families understand recent rapid changes in the sciences of cancer, working with researchers and clinicians. The National Institute for Health Research is working with social scientists on patients' experience of community hospitals; the Medical Research Council funds sociologists to investigate factors behind poor sleep patterns. For the Home Office, 'science' means engineers and criminologists working together with manufacturers to make cars more difficult to steal. The Keeping Warm in Later Life project melds knowledge about income, housing design, boilers and the expertise of health visitors. Without a better grasp of *people*, technological advances may be frustrated or blocked, and fail to realise their potential.

In the next cycle of research assessment, as David Willetts, the former minister for higher education and science said, 'cross-disciplinary working will need greater recognition'.[7] We recommend that funding councils allow researchers to submit outputs to more than one assessment panel, to support interdisciplinary ways of working. There will be important lessons to draw from the funding councils' evaluation of REF 2014 and the review of the role of metrics in research assessment.

THE SCIENCE OF SCIENCE

Within any strategy for science and innovation, social science plays a dual role. Social science is embedded *in science*. Its pursuit of knowledge must be supported along with other disciplines. But social science also provides understanding of how science and innovation work: *the science of science*. Social scientists are establishing the links between spending on research and education and GDP growth,[8] and how GDP should be defined and measured in the light of changing ideas about wellbeing.[9]

Innovation in the life and physical sciences and in software and machines depends on parallel innovation in socio-economic processes for its application and exploitation. Research and development encompasses organisational capital, which the government's science and innovation strategy recognises as 'an area of particular strength in the UK', in a £25.5 billion market.[10] We urge the Treasury and HMRC to examine the way the R&D tax regime recognises social-science-derived innovations in organisational processes. If 'commercialisation of insights and inventions has been historically weak in the UK',[11] the application of social-science-derived thinking and practice in firms, in the training of managers and in industrial 'clusters', is vital in strengthening the link between innovation and exploitation. New ways of working, of engaging staff, of firing the imagination of producers, entrepreneurs and consumers are invaluable in a service economy such as the UK's. They are the province of social science.

In talking about the prospects for 'Graphene City', Luke Georghiou, vice-president for research and innovation at the University of Manchester, urges analysis of the 'centrifugal forces' attracting investment to London and the South East of England.[12] Without models and explanations for flows of capital and employment, technological and scientific development may be stymied.

INNOVATION

If innovation 'is still conceived overwhelmingly in technological rather than in organisational or social terms the notion of social innovation has gained some prominence'.[13] 'A better understanding of how the science and innovation system contributes to economic success, and increased recognition of the complexity and connectivity in the commercialisation process has led to a more holistic and multidimensional approach to policy-making'.[14] Innovation is about new ideas and attitudes and about new ways of doing things in finance, retail and office processes.

The UK spends less on R&D than comparable countries but it's not just new physical products that are important; 'most innovation occurs within institutions ... better understanding of psychology and behaviour can itself lead to valuable innovation'.[15] Through initiatives such as the Gateway to Research, the National Centre for Universities and Business and the Catapult Centres, commercial developments will emerge from sharper understanding of the processes by which technologies are sold, invested in, adapted and propagated. Innovation is a social process.

CASE STUDY

Better understanding of the 'knowledge context' within which firms operate will help translate R&D into products and profits. Social scientists are evaluating 'clusters' – for example, in ultra-low-emission vehicle construction or television and online animation. Study of public values and attitudes is vital, too, especially when innovation prompts uncertainties and concerns, as with genetically modified crops or shale gas extraction. Innovation is increasingly understood not as a race to optimise a single pathway but a collaborative process for exploring different options and trajectories. Andy Stirling points out how global industries are now growing around once-marginal technologies such as wind turbines and super-energy-efficiency buildings that owe their origin to work by grassroots social movements objecting to mainstream technologies.[16] Mariana Mazzucato's study of Apple and the iPhone highlights how much the success and profitability of private companies often depend on defence and other government spending.[17]

Social science feeds a growing evidence base on the role of the state in supporting R&D. Jonathan Haskel established that investment in intangible knowledge has greater productivity-enhancing effects than previously thought, and that the largest benefits to general R&D and economic growth arise from research sponsored by the research councils.[18]

Nesta, which changed its status from a public body to a charity in 2012, has become a valued broker and synthesiser of research and practice in the UK and elsewhere, understanding that advances in technology and knowledge and the processes by which they are applied are fundamentally social phenomena.

BUDGETING FOR SCIENCE

Capacity to innovate depends on research. The UK has an enviable reputation as the producer of first-rate research. With less than 1 per cent of the global population and only 4 per cent of the world's researchers, the UK accounts for 10 per cent of article downloads, 12 per cent of citations and 16 per cent of the world's most highly-cited articles (where it is second only to the United States). Such comparative advantage – to which social science makes a large contribution – must be maintained.

Knowledge underpins the UK's growth potential; productivity depends on sustaining the 'base' through the Science Budget. The 2015 spending review should ring-fence the budget for science and innovation and pledge real terms growth of at least 10 per cent over the lifetime of the next parliament. This is an ambitious figure. But the social science evidence says such investment is essential to keeping the UK competitive.

This additional funding should be dedicated to interdisciplinary research and cross-research-council and cross-disciplinary programmes. Sir Paul Nurse has been commissioned to report on the research councils. We urge the review to recognise the indispensable contribution of social science to cross-disciplinary, problem-focussed research, to push further strategic coordination between the research councils and to build on the 2014 Triennial Review. The Academy of Social Sciences will be presenting evidence to the Nurse Review, citing the ESRC's impressive record in instigating and delivering cross-research-council and cross-science working, as the Triennial Review recognised.[19]

We urge the review to recognise the indispensable contribution of social science to the challenges ahead and its central place in supporting and leading cross-disciplinary, problem-focussed research. Ageing is an example of an issue (and opportunity) that involves medicine, technology, history and the humanities as well as all the social sciences. Its dimensions include labour market participation and pensions, and also family structures and housing design, the institutional borders of the NHS and local government, and the subjective experience and capacities of older people and their relatives.

Social science capital spending is vital. We welcome the recognition of social science in the government's 'roadmap' for capital investment and urge the next government to continue support (with both revenue and capital funding) for the internationally acclaimed birth cohort and longitudinal studies.

Social science contributes to growth by promoting institutional effectiveness. For example, studies establish strong links between pupil background and household income, and attainment at school, health and future earnings. These social facts and causal explanations can be put to use by policymakers; they also matter to teachers, governors, local authorities and, in England, chairs of academy chains. Lessening variation in pupil and school performance could, in aggregate, increase per capita output, pushing up GDP growth.

Social science provides evidence on taxation, benefits, attitudes and incentives: informed policy and political debate depend on it. Growth is not given or necessarily consensual. Choices must be made, about the balance of public and private, taxation and spending, freedom and constraint and about where and to whose benefit. Social science supplies context and helps us locate ourselves.

THE ESRC CONTRIBUTION

In the words of Jane Elliott, chief executive of the ESRC, social science helps us know 'more about ourselves, the families, communities and societies we are part of and the institutions that we work within'. An example is The Future of the UK and Scotland, a programme of research, synthesis and dissemination to help the independence referendum and debate. 'The programme illustrates not just the value but the diversity of the social sciences – including resources on immigration policy, higher education, welfare, defence and security, business, currency and the constitution'.[20]

The ESRC has been successful in stewarding public money, responding to national challenges and priorities while respecting the autonomy of researchers. It must be equipped to respond to the challenges up to 2020 described in this report, including innovation in collecting and analysing new forms of data.

The government's strategy commends 'agility'. The ESRC deserves praise for the speed with which it launched a programme of research and dissemination to inform thinking about the future of the UK and Europe, and its swift response in initiating projects on consumer and business data.

Within the science budget, the ESRC has a strong case in arguing how, after four years of 'flat cash', the international recognition won by UK social science over recent years is in jeopardy. Receiving only 6 per cent of research council funding, it supports excellent and, in several disciplines, world-class research. Resources available for social science research have been relatively squeezed. In 2013–14, the proportion of grant applications gaining funding was 25 per cent, below the average success rate of 28 per cent across the research councils.[21]

In the 2015 spending review, the ESRC's share of the research council budget must better reflect its value for money, support for excellence and promotion of impact, as attested in the 2014 REF.

THE SOCIAL SCIENCE ECOSYSTEM

The ESRC is a part of, and helps maintain, a system of knowledge creation, exchange, training and education. These parts are interdependent and we encourage policymakers to understand and support these mutual dependencies.

The UK labour market has a stock of nearly two million graduates with social science training. They form a large proportion of the workforce in business, education, government and the third sector. They advise on children's use of the internet; they measure the public acceptability of high-speed railways; they help insurers understand the changing contours of risk; they measure and refine the Barnett formula; they chart the changing economics of care within households.

An example of the social scientist as practitioner is Betsy Stanko, head of evidence and insight in the Mayor of London's Office for Policing and Crime. She was formerly an assistant director with the Metropolitan Police Service, applying insights into crime – notably domestic violence – gained from her own and others' academic research.

An example of policy relevance is the finding from Understanding Society, the continuous large-scale study of households, on the increasing value of care given by grandparents. It has increased in notional value by 87 per cent in a decade.[22]

The ecosystem includes 500,000 people with social science postgraduate degrees doing planning and analysis in firms and public bodies; they are employed in marketing, strategy and general management; they produce and exploit socio-economic data on households, consumers and travel-to-work areas. An example: the Department of Health is investing £5 million in the Cambridge Behaviour and Health Research Unit because it sees that the effectiveness of medical interventions depends on organisation, staff attitudes and patient involvement.

Commercial opinion polling exchanges methodological insights with academic investigators of voting and attitudes. Carolyn McCall, chief executive of easyJet, sponsors the Consumer Data Research Centre: its geo-demographic mapping tells the airline about its customers' travel patterns, use of services, access to airports and carbon consumption. At WPP, Sir Martin Sorrell uses knowledge derived from social science methods: 'Understanding consumers, including corporates and how their purchase and media habits are changing is increasingly critical'.[23]

Consultants – RAND, McKinsey, PricewaterhouseCoopers and others – process and apply social science knowledge and concepts. The Treasury, along with other departments of state, rely on the social science ecosystem to supply recruits and to generate knowledge about the economy, banking and public finance, which is deployed internally and by the Bank of England and the Office for Budget Responsibility. Outside government, charities and philanthropic foundations – for example, the Joseph Rowntree Foundation with its £320 million endowment and the Children's Society with £15 million in public service contracts – realise their missions through social science skills and methods.

Figure 2a   The numbers of students in UK universities, by discipline groups

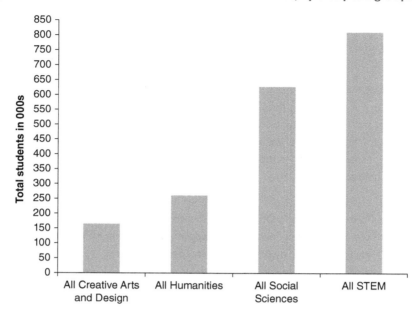

Figure 2b   The numbers of academic staff in UK universities, by discipline groups

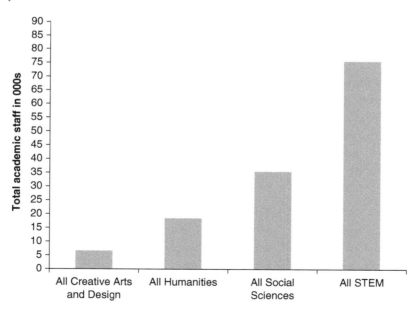

Source: Bastow et al., *The Impact of the Social Sciences*, SAGE, 2014, p. 7

Learned societies are integral to this infrastructure; they publish journals, support school teaching and contribute to the UK's 'soft power'. For example, the Regional Studies Association draws its members from 67 countries; a quarter of the Royal Statistical Society's membership is based outside the UK, as are a fifth of the members of the British Educational Research Association; the Royal Geographical Society with the Institute of British Geographers has affiliated branches in Singapore and Hong Kong. They train, advance knowledge, oversee examinations and disseminate new ideas.

QUALITY NETWORKS

The health of these networks depends on a pipeline of social science degree holders moving to undertake master's courses then flowing into PhD programmes. Non-UK nationals with UK PhDs represent an important source of high-quality recruitment to UK social science.

The REF 2014 results[24] demonstrated again the high quality of UK social science, its central place in delivering impact and the esteem for individual institutions with a social science mission, notably the LSE and the London Business School, which were ranked joint top on the quality of their outputs. The dual support for research should be maintained, recognising the critical role of QR funds in maintaining excellence and diversity in social science. University leaders and social scientists must ensure, within individual universities, that QR money intended to support social science reaches its target.

SOCIAL SCIENCE IS 'DISCIPLINED CURIOSITY'

Dual support is a means of supporting *diversity of approaches*; the social sciences offer varied ways of understanding and measuring human behaviour and activity. But the common aim is getting inside the life of firms, households and individuals, and capturing trends and patterns. We call this report the 'business of people' in the belief that there is deep unity among the disciplines.

A decade ago David Rhind chaired an inquiry on behalf of the Academy of Social Sciences (then called the Academy of Learned Societies in the Social Sciences).[25] It described social science as *disciplined curiosity about the arrangements by which people live together*. *Discipline* means intellectual standards and attested methods (such as citation protocols and sampling error) policed by the professions of psychology, economics, geography, sociology, anthropology and the other disciplines they collaborate and share insights with, as well as by lawyers, historians and accountants. *Applied curiosity* widens and deepens bodies of knowledge about markets, states and institutions, and about groups, attitudes and behaviour.

Companies are employing more social scientists for a good reason. Training in the 'business of people' imbues a vital 21st century attribute: seeing the world as others do and allowing for the possibility that others may see what we have missed. That can imply going backwards in order to move forwards; social science has an open frontier with history and Nick Crafts can enlighten today's and tomorrow's debates about debt and comparative advantage by looking over the 20th century, recalculating the economic impact of the First World War and the state borrowing required to pay for it.[26]

Social science is distinguished from other disciplined curiosity by the tension between its analytical thrust and everyday understanding. Unlike, say, physicists, we report on and conceptualise *shared* lived reality; the public, political parties and politicians may find social science observations uncomfortable. But our mission is to probe the space between what 'common sense' perceives and what measurement and analysis say in pursuit of clarification, classification and explanation.

For example, the Rural Economy and Land Use Programme queried the common assumption that importing foodstuffs from across the globe was unsustainable: it found 'food miles' did not after all match perceived environmental impact.[27] Ipsos MORI – the UK division of an international social-science-based company with a £650 million turnover – regularly allows us to confront the gaps between what people say, what they do and what they say they do.

Because of this, social science has a special obligation to disseminate, market and unpack its findings in the sight and hearing of its subjects. Social scientists do relatively better at outreach than colleagues from the natural sciences and humanities; a higher proportion of grant receivers in social sciences are undertaking research inspired by the users of research.[28]

HANDY NARRATIVES

Social science supplies what Sir Paul Collier calls 'handy narratives' and readily digestible theories in miniature to help the public and policymakers come to terms with the world.[29] Examples of these framing and interpretive devices include globalisation, social mobility and austerity, also 'the Nordic model', networks, systemic risk and diversity. These notions become prisms, or what Daniel Kahneman calls heuristics – procedures that help find adequate, though often imperfect, answers to difficult questions.[30] Everyday terms – money, credit, the family, Britishness – need regularly to be decoded and recalibrated.

Urban forms and futures are the focus of policymakers' and corporate attention as, in England, attention has shifted to prospects for Greater Manchester and other northern conurbations. Cities may be 'innately complex', according to a Government Office for Science Foresight review,[31] but social scientific analysis is setting out the conditions, indicators and models for running them successfully. On social scientists depend many of the 32,000 enterprises involved in urban innovation in the UK, working with government and city authorities on fiscal devolution and regeneration.

But it is striking, says the Chair of the Royal Society of Arts City Growth Commission, Jim O'Neill, how few major companies are based outside London and how talent 'flows into universities around the country but then funnels into London after graduation'.[32] The remedy may be tying cities to the wider growth and innovation agenda, reconcentrating research and students in non-London institutions.

The late Sir Peter Hall, a social science visionary, spoke years ago of 'creating an extraordinary new urban form … a totally new edge city around a high-speed train station'. It came to pass and his successors are now working on innovations in land use, getting the most from High Speed Two, 'garden cities', New Towns and the fiscal basis of development. The 'smart city' – the subject of an RCUK cross-disciplinary initiative – will use reams of data generated in urban life to improve transport and land use. The UK is well placed to prosper in the global market for emerging city technologies; within the next decade the market could be worth £200 billion a year, according to a study by the Future Cities Catapult and Arup.[33]

PART II
THINKING AHEAD

THE NEXT WESTMINSTER PARLIAMENT AND BEYOND

The audience for this report includes MPs, ministers, shadow ministers and their advisers; their stock in trade depends on social science. Politics is suffused with techniques and evidence derived from the study of government, parties and public participation. The apparatus of politics depends on the social science ecosystem – including the continuing flow of investment in research and training.

Political self-understanding matters; it is a precondition of democracy. The Commons' Political and Constitutional Reform Committee turns to Ron Johnston of the University of Bristol for his expertise on parliamentary boundaries. John Curtice is a fixture in television and radio election coverage and sits in a rich tradition leading back among others to Sir Roger Jowell, founder of NatCen social research, and Sir David Butler. To understand the rise of the UK Independence Party, Robert Ford and Matthew Goodwin's *Revolt on the Right* draws on a pool of empirical studies of parties and politics in the UK and internationally.[34]

Knowledge and data can help avoid 'blunders'.[35] Social science methods and disciplines underpin scrutiny and evaluation of policies. The pursuit of effectiveness and better value for money in government rests on cost–benefit analysis and a battery of tools and techniques worked up within social science and across its boundaries with accountancy, epidemiology and operational research and statistics.

Leadership (the subject of intense inquiry by social scientists) is also on display in firms, charities, public bodies, the Bank of England and advertising agencies. These and other organisations need to know what is happening 'out there' in order to locate themselves strategically within markets, regulatory environments, policy streams and social trends. Social scientific analysis precedes and accompanies strategy. It helps decide when and where to sell; the shape and size of audiences; who might give when charitable donations are solicited and how to regulate behaviour without perverse consequences.

A strategy for knowledge from 2015 onwards

Over the next few pages we present examples of social science confronting the challenges the UK will face over the next few years. These illustrate an impressive commitment that merits greater prominence in the government's plan for growth and innovation. We need more strategic thinking about ways in which different forms of knowledge and expertise can be combined. In its *Evidence Strategy* the Department of Environment, Food and Rural Affairs (Defra) said 'it will be vital to coordinate all our evidence activities by working in a more joined-up way. That means working better within government and with partners across a range of organisations'.[36] We echo this with a call for more coordination between the ESRC, other research councils, business, philanthropic research funders and international bodies, but also government itself as the prime commissioner of data and analysis.

Here are abbreviated examples of social science addressing the future, around the themes of growth, behaviour, security and social dynamics. Visit our website for a fuller account of these people and programmes: www.campaignforsocialscience.org.uk/businessofpeople

Going for growth

The backdrop to this report is almost a decade of crisis, recession and recovery. In response, research seeks to capture the finance sector's contribution to productivity and growth, for example Donald MacKenzie's 'sociology of algorithms'; also to retailing, 'big box' warehouses and the fate of the high street.

The Centre for Urban and Regional Development Studies is mapping new travel-to-work areas, reflecting more employees working non-standard hours. Through research on small and medium enterprises (SMEs) and their access to R&D and credit we are finding out more about this vital sector and the ESRC is proposing a longitudinal £10 million study, which would uncover reasons for SMEs' birth, death and survival over time. Among a multitude of studies of the real lives of firms, Bridget Hutter has shown how they negotiate compliance with regulation and Tommaso Valletti how regulating one price (the termination charge for a mobile connection) leads phone companies to raise others.

Performance and capacity

Social scientists specify the conditions for effective governance in firms, charities and government agencies. The students they train form the backbone of the human resources and occupational psychology functions across organisations. They supply practical advice: the University of Bath Centre for Research in Strategic Purchasing and Supply helped the NHS save £250 million on the purchase price of hearing aids.

Reporting on airport capacity in the South East of England, Sir Howard Davies, former director of the LSE, relies on studies on airport connectivity as the driver of economic growth, on low carbon transport alternatives and on public attitudes to noise and pollution. Social researchers are employed by train operating companies, engineering partnerships and sustainable transport lobby groups. On the tracks, psychologists collaborated with Bombardier in designing a new train protection and warning system for drivers' cabs. On the roads, or rather the pavements, in a road safety programme being cited across the world, James Thomson and colleagues help children acquire 'kerbcraft'.

Social science provides the evidence for when and how interventions in the early years of a child's life are highly likely to secure better outcomes later in life. The effects of neo-natal screening and breastfeeding are being modelled and costed; social scientists work with the NHS in designing and putting in place programmes to change mothers' attitudes and behaviour. We know how to make children's immunisation programmes more effective and can calculate the costs and benefits of breakfast clubs in deprived areas.

Such studies underpin a broad 'invest to save' proposition: actions now could cut future public spending on welfare, health and criminal justice (savings of £200,000 per child have been estimated in one anti-social-behaviour programme). Research for the Early Intervention Foundation (EIF) shows that home visiting or individual therapy interventions have the strongest evidence of effectiveness, compared with group-based ones. Developing 'executive function' skills at the ages of three and four helps children to learn, take part and make friends at nursery and school, with cascading effects on their subsequent chances of success.

On domestic violence and abuse, the EIF assesses preventive programmes for children and young people and goes on to advocate specific actions by government and other agencies; these include a targeted intervention to build the ability of adolescent parents to carry on relationships. We can measure the connection between childcare and nursery quality and children's school success – a connection that applies independently of the socio-economic background of the child. Emla Fitzsimons and colleagues running the Millennium Cohort Study found children of married couples are less likely to demonstrate problem behaviour. The positive effect of fathers' involvement with their children's upbringing has been measured; similarly grandparent care is strongly related to child wellbeing – a finding influential in the drafting of the Children and Families Act 2014.

Behaving better

Economic and social characteristics are now being linked with the wealth of biological and medical data in UK Biobank. We are beginning to explore the relationship between the genome and income, background and upbringing, with potentially huge consequences for policy and public spending. Neuroscience joins with social science in understanding brain function and behaviour in classrooms, teaching effectiveness and school–home interaction.

The UK's 2013–18 cross-government antimicrobial resistance strategy wants to apply genomic technology to improve surveillance of disease outbreaks, along with social science analysis of clinician, media, patient and government attitudes and practice, 'aimed at raising awareness and encouraging behaviour change'.[37] Important social science research is carried on within government. The recent finding by the DfE that overall 14 per cent of young people receive additional private tuition (24 per cent in London) is deeply relevant to policy and school evaluation.[38]

Firms and government agencies try to change behaviour through financial incentives, advertising, coercion and 'nudging'. Recent examples include re-wording letters from HMRC and enrolment in pension schemes. Research by Jane Millar and colleagues influenced the design of tax credits, which have increased labour market participation and, as evaluated by the IFS, helped equalise incomes.

On ageing, social science is sceptical about decline in family integration or deterioration in the performance of older people as paid workers. Researchers are monitoring the safeguarding of older people and, on behalf of the Department for Work and Pensions (DWP), modelling the effects of raising the state retirement age. The ESRC and the Engineering and Physical Sciences Research Council (EPSRC) are together investing £8.3 million in how the built environment encourages physical activity and wellbeing in both care homes and the wider urban environment. Healthy life expectancy may fall back because of obesity: Susan Michie and colleagues at the UCL Centre for Behaviour Change are among those contributing to understanding physical activity and healthfulness.

Securing society

Social scientists are working on gangs, organised and 'honour' crime, child abuse and trafficking. Social scientists study untoward events such as flooding and investigate victims and emergency response. The social science advisory panel convened by Defra and the Department of Energy and Climate Change (DECC) assesses threats to biosecurity from pests and plant disease, and models how the media, business and public might respond in the event of an outbreak. Social scientists estimate what a healthier diet would mean for land use, leading to fewer cattle being raised, and how uplands communities might be affected as the ovine economy changes.

The UK in the world

Social science underpins diplomacy and defence, as conventional definitions of domestic and foreign give way to a more integrated understanding of the UK in the world. Anthropologists and others are on the front line in Afghanistan and Iraq; they help analyse internet traffic, placing terrorism in a wider context of minority communities, discrimination, geographical isolation and economic opportunity. Social research helps understand radicalisation, underpinning the Prevent strategy.

The Royal United Services Institute works with the MoD and companies to link defence planning assumptions and the development of a sustainable structure for UK armed forces with projections of the UK's place in the world. And nowadays social science also studies the converse: the place of the world in the UK. The Centre on Migration, Policy and Society examines the flow of people across boundaries, including nation state boundaries; with the Centre for Research and Analysis of Migration, it assesses patterns of settlement and the impact of migrants on labour markets.

Social scientists are extensively used by the Department for International Development to design and implement aid programmes, and by the World Bank and other international bodies (reflected in Sylvia Walby's UNESCO Chair in Gender Research). Projects range from macro-prudential regulation in middle-income countries to pensions in Tamil Nadu. Social scientists report on temporary workers in the South Pacific islands, on remittance flows between the UK and Somalia, agricultural subsidies in Malawi, post-conflict reconciliation in central Africa and war-displaced communities in Sudan. Trade and partnerships with China depend on understanding its society and markets. Stephen Tsang, head of the School of Contemporary Chinese Studies at the University of Nottingham, uses the concept of 'consultative Leninism' to understand politics in the People's Republic. Lancaster University's China Catalyst Programme focuses on Guangdong, aiming to help UK companies to trade there. Fulong Wu of UCL works with city authorities in China on housing for rural migrants.

The UK's capacity for interdisciplinary research is a crucial asset in any collaborative venture, and the Newton Fund should prioritise projects which bring together UK natural scientists, social scientists and engineers to work with their counterparts in emerging economies, such as China, India and Brazil, on shared social and environmental challenges. We encourage wider appreciation of social scientists' success in international research competition.

Economic and social dynamics

Through longitudinal studies, social scientists have established the likelihood of young people from poorer backgrounds rising to prestigious positions. The quality and rigour of analysis of social mobility in the UK is admired internationally. John Goldthorpe and colleagues see little evidence that social mobility is declining but do detect increasing risk of downward mobility. The chances of a child with a higher-professional or managerial father ending up in a similar position rather than in a manual position are up to 20 times greater than the same chances for a child whose father is a manual worker.

Social science lays out conditions for happiness and wellbeing; these include a sense of belonging, trust, social cohesion and access to justice. Sue Heath and colleagues at the

Morgan Centre for Research into Everyday Lives show how kinship and relationships are changing wellbeing inside families. In their advocacy of cognitive therapies for people suffering from depression and anxiety, Lord Richard Layard and David Clark have pushed public policy in a new direction and made clinical practice more (cost) effective. The life's work of Sir Cary Cooper, Chair of the Academy of Social Sciences, has been connecting organisational success to the psychological health and wellbeing of staff.

Data

Social scientists – for example at the Oxford Internet Institute – are joining with mathematicians and engineers to mine the data generated as people spend more time in digital contexts. New neighbourhood-level statistics of the kind being put together by Dave Martin are of use to school chains and voluntary organisations. Data collected by the DWP and HMRC is now being exploited. With the launch of the ESRC's Big Data Network, opportunities beckon better to understand patterns in retail trading.

Data sets are a form of capital investment; the longitudinal studies and the census are national assets, without which it would be impossible to measure social change, mobility or the significance of migration. The innovative Life Study aims to chart the life course of 80,000 babies born in 2014–15. These data sets appreciate as value as time elapses. Follow up in the early years of children from the 2014–15 Life Study would be immensely valuable; many Life Study children will live to 100 years or more, presenting unparalleled opportunity for study and policy. But during the next six years, the Life Study and other cohorts will need further investment of £60 million.

Whitehall departments and the UK Statistics Authority/ONS are also major investors in data infrastructure. Sustaining their R&D budgets is vital and could be better coordinated. The Chair of the UK Data Forum, Tim Holt, is right to regret the 'fractured nature of decision making' around the commissioning and exploitation of the UK's outstanding data sets.[39]

We urge the next UK government to pick up the policies prepared by the Cabinet Office to create a statutory presumption in favour of sharing deidentified public data for research purposes.

A condition of the successful exploitation of these data riches is the expansion of quantitative and methodological capacity among social scientists. Better training for social science undergraduates is advancing with the £15.5 million Quantitative Methods Programme, supported by the Nuffield Foundation, the ESRC and the university funding councils. We are committed to ensuring that a social science degree becomes, even more than today, a passport to data understanding and exploitation. Building on Q-Step, social science education must increasingly equip the next generation of researchers with quantitative techniques, the capacity to acquire and analyse new forms of data, and the disposition to work collaboratively with other scientists.

PART III
THE BUSINESS OF SOCIAL SCIENCE

THE ENTERPRISE OF SOCIAL SCIENCE

Policymakers' and parliamentarians' appetite for evidence from analysis and experiment has grown. The coalition minister for policy, Oliver Letwin, talks of the need for 'people who champion effective use of social research and social science at the very highest levels in government'.[40] Executives in the financial, energy, transport as well as retail sectors demand better intelligence on consumers and behaviour; internet-based companies are now appointing chief social science officers. The third sector turns to social science to help measure impact and to persuade donors of their effectiveness.

One symbol of this confidence in the future is the opening of the Social Science Research Park at Cardiff University's new £300-million campus at Maindy Park, the sort of space, says university president Colin Riordan, 'where people say "I want to do my business there because the understanding and innovation is there"'.[41]

International reviews benchmark UK social science as world class, second only to the United States, with a growing share of the world output of academic papers.[42] UK geography is ranked number one worldwide; economics, psychology, politics and international studies are second only to the United States on several measures; social anthropology leads in work on kinship and complex organisations; sociology is at 'the international forefront' with particular strength in science and technology studies.

Internationally, social scientists extensively cite UK research. The UK talks to the world, giving it influence greater than researcher numbers (or funding) would imply; the same applies

Figure 3   Estimated citation impact of articles in the social sciences by country

	Citation per article	Field-weighted citation impact
UK	2.42	1.15
US	2.25	1.05
Canada	2.20	1.05
Italy	1.64	0.98
Germany	1.68	0.93
Japan	1.12	0.73
France	1.10	0.66
China	0.75	0.58

Source: Elsevier, 'International Comparative Performance of the UK Research Base – 2011', A report prepared for the Department for Business, Innovation and Skills, October 2011

to UK publishing in social science fields. Half of all international students in the UK are taking courses in the social sciences, which is a higher proportion than for any other disciplinary grouping. Non-UK students in the social sciences at UK universities number over 150,000; most leave after their studies but retain personal and professional connections, which are of sustained value to the UK. The next government should keep international students out of any targets to reduce net migration and reintroduce the option for non-EU graduates to stay in the UK to work for two years.

UK SOCIAL SCIENCE – SOME DIMENSIONS

One estimate puts the gross value of UK social science at £25 billion, about half the size of the motor manufacturing industry.[43] The professional research and evidence market is worth £3 billion, employing some 60,000 people, according to estimates from PricewaterhouseCoopers.[44] UK companies spend nearly 1 per cent of GDP on marketing, equivalent to £16 billion. The Carnegie Trust, Barrow Cadbury, Esmée Fairbairn and other endowments dedicate many millions to social science studies. Whitehall and the devolved administrations commission research, the latter worth around £4 million a year, paying for in-house researchers and surveys. Local authorities across the UK use social research as they plan housing and provision of school places.

A full accounting would assess 'goodwill' and intellectual property contained in the social science knowledge and methods being put to use across the economy. This calculus of value would also put a price on ideas and practical innovation in such areas as supply chain innovation, reshaping attitudes to the employability of older people, the scale of viable farming, supermarket price-cut deals, surviving cancer, preventing suicides on railways and decision making by people with dementia.

Some 630,000 students are enrolled on undergraduate and postgraduate courses in the social sciences in UK universities, compared with some 800,000 in STEM subjects. About 35,500 academic staff teach and research in social science against some 75,000 in STEM. The respective ratios of staff to students in universities are 1:19 and 1:11. University social science receives £851 million in research grants and contracts (of which £594 million comes from funding and research councils) while STEM subjects receive £4,777 million, £3,083 million from the councils.

Social science academics reach out to business, the public and government to a slightly greater extent than academics in STEM subjects, who have greater purchase on the media and the professions.

University STEM departments are more strongly linked to big companies and to small and medium enterprises, but business and management has strong links to international

Figure 4   The percentage of links from STEM and social science departments to different industrial and commercial sectors

	STEM Sciences		Social Sciences	
	Manufacturing and primary sector	Services	Services	Manufacturing and primary Sector
ICT and technology	25	20	12	5
Industrial, engineering and utilities	17	6	4	8
Bioscience	10	0	0	1
Consulting and business services	5	6	12	3
Financial services and insurance	0	1	9	2
Retail and products	6	2	10	2
Media, marketing, and creative	0	2	14	1
Law and legal services	0	0	8	0
Other (including professional associations)	0	0	9	0
% Sub-totals for sectors	**63**	**37**	**78**	**22**
Total for each discipline group	*100%*		*100%*	
N of links for totals	*281*		*417*	

Source: Bastow et al., *The Impact of the Social Sciences*, SAGE, 2014, p. 123

companies, as does law. Social science academics are, correspondingly, more strongly connected to government, the NHS, international organisations and agencies than STEM colleagues.

Social science students take their degrees into all areas of employment, but predominantly into management, education, research and the professions. Employers say they want well-rounded graduates with strong analytical skills. Many courses might supply these. But recruiters add that they want people with imagination and social skills. Social science degrees supply these too.

When traced three and a half years after graduating, one in eight social science students are in health and social work and one in 14 in the wider public sector. One in 12 are in management positions, one in five in professional/scientific/technical jobs and one in 14 in finance and insurance.

Figure 5   Employment industries, by degree subject group

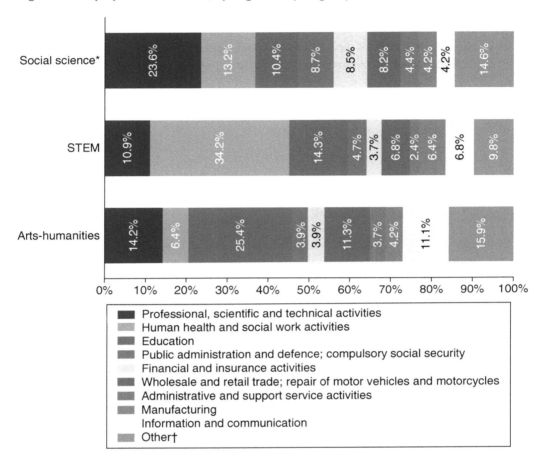

*Excludes education graduates, whose profile is markedly different: 78.3 per cent of education graduates work in education; 1.1 per cent in professional, scientific and technical activities; 9.7 per cent in human health and social work activities; 2.9 per cent in public administration, defence and compulsory social security; 2.6 per cent in wholesale and retail trade and repair of motor vehicles and motorcycles; 0.7 per cent in financial and insurance activities; 0.5 per cent in administrative and support service activities; 0.8 per cent in manufacturing; 0.4 per cent in information and communication; 2.7 per cent in other.

† 'Other' includes the following industries: Accommodation and food service activities; Construction; Real estate activities; Arts, entertainment and recreation; Transport and storage; Other service activities; Electricity, gas, steam and air conditioning supply; Mining and quarrying; Water supply, sewerage, waste management and remediation activities; Agriculture, forestry and fishing; Activities of extraterritorial organisations and bodies; Activities of households as employers, and undifferentiated goods- and services-producing activities of households for own use.

Source: 'What Do Social Science Graduates Do?' A report by the Campaign for Social Science, October 2013

Social science graduates form about 15 per cent of the total graduate population of 10.5 million. Those with social science postgraduate qualifications are most evident among business and public service professionals, in management and administration, in health and social welfare, sales and customer service. Some 600,000 social science graduates are in public administration, education and health, and half a million or so in banking and finance.

In schools, teachers of geography, social studies, economics and some general studies form about 12 per cent of the professional workforce (that is 27,000 English state secondary school teachers).

SOCIAL SCIENCE PEOPLE

Social scientists contribute directly as individuals. Government departments and agencies turn to experts both for advice and to conduct specific inquiries; some (the Bank of England for example) recruit many for full- and part-time roles.

Here are some examples of recent public service social scientists. It's not so much the distinction of these individuals as the fact that they belong to the ecosystem; the talent pool that produces them would dry up without continuing support from training and research council and other grants.

Sir John Hills examined fuel poverty for DECC. His colleague from the LSE, Sir Julian Le Grand, led a review of children's services in Birmingham and heads the taskforce on mutuals. Carol Tannahill is seconded from the Glasgow Centre for Population Health as chief social policy adviser to the Scottish Government. In Wales, Dame Teresa Rees, formerly commissioner for the Equal Opportunities Commission, has advised BT, and was a member of the BBC audience council among several appointments. Dame Kate Barker carried out a major review of housing supply under the previous government; recently she chaired the King's Fund commission on the future of health and social care. Tanya Byron, specialist in child and adolescent psychology, conducted the review entitled Safer Children in a Digital World. David Halpern entered public service and helped found what is now the Behavioural Insights Unit.

Huw Williams, director of the Centre for Clinical Neuropsychology Research, carried out studies on behalf of the Department of Health and the Office of the Children's Commissioner. Rory O'Connor, professor of health psychology at the University of Glasgow, advises the Scottish government on suicide prevention. Matthew Oakley, former head of economics and social policy at Policy Exchange, now at Which?, conducted an independent review of Jobseeker's Allowance sanctions for the DWP.

John Kay, former head of the Saïd Business School at Oxford, was commissioned by BIS to examine investment in UK equity markets and its impact on the long-term performance of UK quoted companies. Sir Andrew Dilnot, now warden of Nuffield College, Oxford, is Chair of the UK Statistics Authority and reported on the costs of social care. The Natural Capital Committee is chaired by Dieter Helm, the University of Oxford economist.

Competition appeals use the skills and experience of the likes of Colin Mayer of the Saïd Business School and John Beath, secretary general of the Royal Economic Society. Social scientists are deployed on the pay review bodies and in the administration of town and country planning. Sir David Metcalf chairs the Home Office Migration Advisory Committee.

On behalf of the DfE, Eileen Munro led a review of child protection. Sir Lawrence Freedman, professor of war studies at King's College, London, was official historian of the Falklands Campaign and serves on the Chilcot inquiry into Britain and the 2003 Iraq War.

The Scottish government convenes a council of economic advisers, which includes Sir James Mirrlees, a Nobel economics prize-winner. The Scottish Science Advisory Council helps the Scottish government's chief scientific adviser, and its members include Sir Ian Diamond, former chief executive of the ESRC. Huw Beynon is a member of the Science Advisory Council for Wales, feeding into the Welsh government through the chief scientific adviser.

We urge more senior social scientists in academic positions and practice to put themselves forward for appointments in government service. The Royal Society has in recent years devised programmes to mentor and support potential recruits to advisory roles. The Academy of Social Sciences is keen to work to develop similar initiatives for social scientists.

SOCIAL SCIENCE AND GOVERNMENT

At Westminster and in the devolved administrations, ministers, elected members and officials are now much more aware of how policy and cost effectiveness can be improved through evidence, scrutiny and evaluation. But relevant knowledge is haphazardly deployed: the use of evidence grounded in research and analysis is intermittent, and what is recognised as 'science' often misses insights from social-science-based analysis.

The chief scientist at Defra (a veterinarian) has noted that over badger culling the big gaps in knowledge and understanding were not about disease transmission or herd behaviour but about public attitudes, land use, property and farming practice. The roll out of 'digital by default' government services depends on much more than technology: it requires better understanding of attitudes and behaviours.

The Prime Minister, Cabinet Secretary and GCSA need a 'chief social scientist' to supply wide social science perspectives on institutions, behaviour and data.

This role should be based within the Government Office for Science (working with the GCSA) or added to the responsibilities of one of the departmental chief scientific advisers.

In addition, we urge more Whitehall departments to appoint candidates from social science backgrounds as their chief scientific advisers, as in the DfE and the Treasury.

Departmental advisory committees should also (as in Defra and DECC) routinely include social scientists, both academics and practitioners. Arm's-length bodies, quangos and local authorities – especially in large cities – should review their use and commissioning of social science knowledge and evidence.

Ministers and representatives and civil servants could be better equipped to commission evidence. It is still rare to find maps of knowledge needs (such as the DfE's) or strategies for evidence (such as Defra's). Research councils connect only ad hoc with departments. There is a long way to go either before existing policies are routinely evaluated or plans checked against evidence, let alone made subject to experiment, piloting or trial.[45] Social science analysis and financial audit, though their subject matter and questions are often similar, tend not to be joined up.

Yet good evidence for policymakers abounds, along with the expertise to apply it. For example, research for the Sutton Trust calibrates the effect of teacher quality. In partnership with the Treasury and HMRC, the IFS is helping design tax operations and policy. The Scottish Government's Centre of Expertise on Climate Change collaborates with social scientists, for example from the University of Strathclyde. The MoD is cooperating with the ESRC in bringing social scientists from universities and the thinktanks together with officials and services staff to scope challenges for the next Strategic Defence Review.

Social scientists are involved both as advisers and witnesses in parliamentary inquiries and their value is now being recognised at Westminster and in the devolved parliaments and assemblies. Thanks to ESRC support, the Parliamentary Office for Science and Technology now includes social science advisers, but more needs to be done to equip representatives for scrutiny and oversight and feed into value for money studies by the National Audit Office and parallel bodies. Social scientific advice to the Westminster parliament and the legislative bodies in the devolved administrations should be further strengthened, as part of broader modernisation of scrutiny and oversight.

Successive reports – most recently from the ESRC's 'knowledge navigators' – say the effectiveness of local authorities could be improved if they had a closer relationship with producers of knowledge, data and analysis, either individually or through their central associations.

Tighter evaluation of policies and how they are delivered is more than ever a precondition of better value for money. Inspired by the National Institute for Health and Care Excellence, What Works centres use social science methods to collect evidence to evaluate and improve performance of government agencies, local authorities and voluntary bodies. National adviser David Halpern, a distinguished social scientist in his own right, says the aim is to offer the best expert assessment to professional service staff or policy commissioners. It's for them to make the final judgement on what to do, weighing up public sentiment and the context of policy as well as the impartial expert view.

The centres sit firmly within the social science ecosystem, relying on long strands of previous work and the continuing capacity of the ESRC and government research commissioners to innovate and back new projects. The seven UK central government centres cover areas where around £200 billion is spent each year. They include the College of Policing Centre for Crime Reduction, the Education Endowment Foundation, the EIF, the Centre for Local Economic Growth, the Centre for Ageing Better (improved quality of life for older people) and the Centre for Wellbeing. In addition there is What Works Scotland, focused on public service improvement, and the Public Policy Institute for Wales, providing advice across the range of Welsh Government competencies in a rolling programme agreed with the First Minister. The centres review existing findings and stimulate new inquiries, disseminating results to decision makers and improving the capacity of government to commission and apply evidence. Among recent findings is the discovery that pupils in a class with a teaching assistant do not, on average, perform better than those in a class with only a teacher; but teaching assistants can have a positive impact if they are trained in specific ways, backed by trials in schools. Another shows how small group tuition can be a cost-effective alternative to one-to-one teaching for struggling pupils. All review existing research findings and stimulate new inquiries, disseminating results to decision makers and improving the capacity of public officials to commission and apply evidence. The Centre for Local Economic Growth found 'the overall measurable effects of major sport and culture projects on a local economy tend not to be large and are more often zero', with wage and income effects usually small and limited to the immediate locality or particular types of worker.

But the What Works centres only 'work' if they are rigorous and intellectually independent. The precondition for their success is the health of the UK social science ecosystem – which depends, we say, on clearer recognition of research strength in official strategy and sustained public investment.

References

1   BIS, 'Our Plan for Growth: Science and innovation – evidence', December 2014, www.gov.uk/government/publications/our-plan-for-growth-science-and-innovation-evidence

2   Government Office for Science, 'Innovation: Managing risk, not avoiding it – Annual report of the Government Chief Scientific Adviser', November 2014, www.gov.uk/government/publications/innovation-managing-risk-not-avoiding-it

3   Besley, Timothy et al., 'Investing for Prosperity: Skills, infrastructure and innovation – Report of the LSE Growth Commission', January 2013, www.lse.ac.uk/researchAndExpertise/units/growthCommission/documents/pdf/LSEGC-Report.pdf

4   House of Commons Public Administration Select Committee, Oral evidence to 'Whitehall: Capacity to address future challenges' inquiry, HC 669, December 9, 2014. See also MoD, 'Global Strategic Trends out to 2045', Fifth Edition, August 2014

5   British Academy, 'Punching our Weight: The humanities and social sciences in public policy making', September 2008, www.britac.ac.uk/policy/punching-our-weight.cfm

6   KPMG website, 'KPMG and Imperial College London form £20 million partnership', July 15, 2014, www.kpmg.com/uk/en/issuesandinsights/articlespublications/newsreleases/pages/kpmg-and-imperial-college-london-form-%C2%A320-million-partnership-to-transform-uk-into-global-leader-in-big-data-analytics.aspx

7   Willetts, David, 'Make assessment more inclusive', *Research Fortnight*, December 18, 2014, p. 10

8   Haskel, Jonathan et al., 'The Economic Significance of the UK Science Base – A report for the Campaign for Science and Engineering', UK Innovation Research Centre, March 2014, www.sciencecampaign.org.uk/?page_id=14040

9   Coyle, Diane, *GDP: A brief but affectionate history*, Princeton University Press, 2014

10 www.gov.uk/government/publications/our-plan-for-growth-science-and-innovation-evidence

11 www.lse.ac.uk/researchAndExpertise/units/growthCommission/home.aspx

12 Times Higher Education, October 16, 2014, p. 8

13 European Science Foundation, 'Science in Society: Caring for our future in turbulent times', June 2013, www.esf.org/fileadmin/Public_documents/Publications/spb50_ScienceInSociety.pdf

14 www.gov.uk/government/publications/our-plan-for-growth-science-and-innovation-evidence

15 Annual report of the Government Chief Scientific Adviser 2014, 'Innovation: Managing risk, not avoiding it – evidence and case studies', November 2014, www.gov.uk/government/publications/innovation-managing-risk-not-avoiding-it

16 See reference 15

17 Mazzucato, Mariana, *The Entrepreneurial State*, Anthem Press, 2013

18 www.sciencecampaign.org.uk/?page_id=14040

19 BIS, 'Triennial Review of the Research Councils, Final Report', April 2014, www.rcuk.ac.uk/media/news/140416/

20 ESRC, *Society Now*, Autumn 2014, p. 27

21 Times Higher Education, November 20, 2014, pp. 6–7

22 Understanding Society, *Insights 2014*, University of Essex, www.understandingsociety.ac.uk/insights2014

23 Market Research Society website, 'UK research market worth over £3bn, says first comprehensive sector review', October 8, 2012, www.mrs.org.uk/article/item/556

24 Research Excellence Framework 2014: The results, December 2014, http://results.ref.ac.uk/

25 Rhind, David, 'Great Expectations: The social sciences in Great Britain', Commission on the Social Sciences, March 2003

26 Crafts, Nicholas, 'Walking wounded: The British economy in the aftermath of World War I', article for VOX, August 27, 2014, www.voxeu.org/article/walking-wounded-british-economy-aftermath-world-war-i

27 Mehra, Melini, 'Food Miles: Should we be buying food from abroad?' presentation for RELU Science Debate, March 17, 2006, www.relu.ac.uk/events/SciWeek2006/Mehra.pdf

28 Bastow, Simon et al., *The Impact of the Social Sciences: How academics and their research make a difference*, SAGE, 2014

29 Collier, Paul, *Exodus: Immigration and multiculturalism in the 21st century*, Penguin, 2013

30 Kahneman, Daniel, *Thinking, Fast and Slow*, Allen Lane, 2011

31 Government Office for Science, 'Future of Cities: Comparative urban governance', WP10, October 2014, www.gov.uk/government/publications/future-cities-comparative-urban-governance

32 Times Higher Education, November 27, 2014, p. 30

33 Catapult Future Cities/Arup, 'UK Capabilities for Urban Innovation', July 2014. See also www.arup.com/smart; Hauser, Hermann, 'Review of the Catapult Network', November 2014, www.gov.uk/government/publications/catapult-centres-hauser-review-recommendations

34 Ford, Robert and Goodwin, Matthew, *Revolt on the Right*, Routledge, 2014

35 King, Anthony and Crewe, Ivor, *The Blunders of our Governments*, Oneworld, 2013

36 Defra, 'Making the Most of our Evidence: A strategy for Defra and its network', June 2014, www.gov.uk/government/publications/evidence-strategy-for-defra-and-its-network

37 Department of Health, 'UK Five Year Antimicrobial Resistance Strategy 2013 to 2018', September 2013, www.gov.uk/government/publications/uk-5-year-antimicrobial-resistance-strategy-2013-to-2018

38 DfE, 'Longitudinal Study of Young People in England: Cohort 2, wave 1 – Research report', November 2014, www.gov.uk/government/publications/longitudinal-study-of-young-people-in-england-cohort-2-wave-1

39 UK Data Forum, 'UK Strategy for Data Resources for Social and Economic Research 2013–2018', July 2013, www.esrc.ac.uk/_images/UKDF-strategy-data-resources_tcm8-26806.pdf

40 Letter to Lord Selborne, Chair of House of Lords Science and Technology Committee, 30th July 2014, www.parliament.uk/documents/lords-committees/science-technology/behaviourchangefollowup/LetwinBehaviourChangeReply20140730.pdf

41 Field, James, 'Cardiff University lights spark for a 'world first'', article for Research Professional, October 8, 2014, www.researchprofessional.com/0/rr/news/uk/universities/2014/10/Cardiff-University-lights-spark-for-a--world-first--.html#sthash.79WfwqmN.dpuf

42 Elsevier, 'International Comparative Performance of the UK Research Base – 2013: A report prepared by Elsevier for the Department for Business, Innovation and Skills (BIS)', SciVal/Elsevier, December 2013, www.gov.uk/government/publications/performance-of-the-uk-research-base-international-comparison-2013

43 Bastow, Simon et al., *The Impact of the Social Sciences*, 2014

44 www.mrs.org.uk/article/item/556

45 National Audit Office, 'Evaluation in Government', December 2013, www.nao.org.uk/report/evaluation-government/

Milton Keynes UK
Ingram Content Group UK Ltd.
UKHW012228020924
447784UK00007B/180